Why Trust the
Bible?

Study Guide

Why Trust the
Bible?

Study Guide

Greg Gilbert

with Alex Duke

∷ CROSSWAY®

WHEATON, ILLINOIS

Contents

Study Guide Preface

"Well, actually . . ."

Has anyone ever said that to you? You say something; they don't agree, and so they begin their rebuttal in which they tell you how it *really* is. People do that a lot with the Bible.

"In the beginning, God created the heavens and the earth" (Gen. 1:1). *Well, actually . . .*

"Male and female he created them" (Gen. 1:27). *Well, actually . . .*

Jesus "came to them, walking on the sea" (Mark 6:48). *Well, actually . . .*

"I do not permit a woman to teach or to exercise authority over a man" (1 Tim. 2:12). *Well, actually . . .*

"It is appointed for man to die once, and after that comes judgment" (Heb. 9:27). *Well, actually . . .*

What about you? Have you ever said "Well, actually" to the Bible?

Five years ago, Greg Gilbert wrote *Why Trust the Bible?* in order to persuade people that trusting the Bible isn't just for dutiful dunces who do what they're told. Nor is trusting the Bible intellectually naïve. In fact, it's quite the opposite. Intellectually honest people have all the evidence they need.

We've written this accompanying study guide for one simple reason: to guide you through *Why Trust the Bible?* The structure is not complicated; the goals are not lofty. It simply walks chapter by chapter through the book, forcing you as the reader to slow down and consider what you've read.

Who's it for? Any Christian will profit both from Greg Gilbert's book and this study guide. It will help give a reason for a hope that Christians have. I trust it would also be useful for curious non-Christians who want to consider the claims of Scripture and, ultimately, the claims of the risen Jesus Christ.

How should you use this study guide? Alone? One-on-one? In small groups? It doesn't matter. We hope older church members will use this to disciple younger church members, and Christians will use it to evangelize non-Christians. Beyond that, who knows? The Lord is honored as his people sow the seed of the gospel. His trustworthy word does not return void.

May God grant many eyes to see, ears to hear, and hearts softened to believe.

Alex Duke
September 2020

1

Don't Believe Everything You Read

Why Trust the Bible? Summary
You can trust the Bible without checking your brain at the door. You can trust the Bible for reasons other than "my parents taught me to" or "my pastor says I should." This introductory chapter explains what kind of trust you can have in the Bible—and what you need to achieve it.

1. Do you trust the Bible? If so, why? If not, why not?

2. What are some bad reasons to trust the Bible? What are some good ones?

3. What did Jesus think about the Old Testament—and why does it matter?

4. The author writes, "It's turtles all the way down for all of us, no matter what you take as your final authority for knowledge" (p. 16). What does he mean? Do you agree with him? Why or why not?

5. In this chapter, the author spends some time talking about presuppositions. What presuppositions do you have?

6. This book is an exercise in "doing history" (p. 19). Why is that a perfectly acceptable approach?

7. What's the "chain of reliability" (pp. 20–21)?

List the five big questions in the chain for determining the reliability of the Bible. (See pages 21–22.)

(1)

(2)

(3)

(4)

(5)

8. What's the difference between "historical confidence" and "mathematical certainty" (pp. 23–24)?

2

Lost in Translation?

Why Trust the Bible? Summary

Do you know what "Μὴ θησαυρίζετε ὑμῖν θησαυροὺς ἐπὶ τῆς γῆς" means? Is it even *possible* to know what "Μὴ θησαυρίζετε ὑμῖν θησαυροὺς ἐπὶ τῆς γῆς" means? Yes, it is, because translation is possible.

1. Why is the question of translation so important?

2. Refer to the Kidspeak illustration on pages 32–33. Give an example of how you've done translation in your own life.

3. If translation is possible, then why are there so many Bible versions? Does the existence of so many translations undermine the claim that translation is possible? Explain why or why not. (See pages 33–40.)

4. Pick out a verse at random, look it up online, and copy down three or four various translations of that random verse below. Do you understand what the biblical author was trying to communicate?

5. What are the two aims of a good Bible translation? (See page 40.)

3

Copies of Copies of Copies of Copies?

Why Trust the Bible? Summary

Some folks say the Bible is riddled with errors, that the book you have at your bedside is so corrupted as to be untrustworthy. But is that really the case? How does the Bible—and the New Testament, in particular—stack up against other ancient literature? The answer to these questions might surprise you.

1. The chapter focuses on the task of transmission. Have you ever given this subject any thought? What would you say to someone if they charged the Bible with just being "a copy of a copy of a copy of a copy"?

2. How many ancient manuscripts and fragments of the New Testament do we have? Why does this enable us to know with high confidence what the originals said?

3. If you were to look at the various antique manuscripts of the Bible we have, you'd notice some differences. Did you know that? Does that lower your confidence of the Bible at your bedside?

4. How long is the gap between the original writers and our earliest surviving copies? Why is this not a big deal? How does this gap compare to other historical documents listed on pages 48 and 49?

5. There are "up to 500,000 variants" in the Bible! (p. 49). What can we say about this audacious claim?

6. The author writes, "Believe it or not, at any given point in the New Testament where variants occur, it is precisely the existence of those variants that allows us to piece together what the original document most likely said" (p. 52). How does this work in practice? How does the "*harder* reading" (p. 55) help us?

7. Have you noticed the footnotes in your Bible that describe different translations? Far from inviting insecurity, these parts of Scripture should encourage you. As the author writes, "There's no conspiracy to pull the wool over anyone's eyes" (p. 57). Use your own or an online study Bible and spend the next 15 minutes looking for these footnotes. What have you learned from this exercise?

4

Are These Really the Books You're Looking For?

Why Trust the Bible? Summary

If you've read or seen *The Da Vinci Code*, you've heard the claim that the Bible's sixty-six books are simply the result of a power struggle in the early church. They're not inspired but victorious.

1. What is a canon? (See page 62.)

2. The author says the idea that there was a conspiracy to arrive at this particular canon is "arrant nonsense" (p. 64). How does he defend himself?

3. Why is the distinction between "choosing" and "receiving" books so vital? (See pages 67–68.)

4. What plausible, historically valid reasons did the authors have for accepting the New Testament canon? List and briefly explain the four main reasons below. (See pages 69–72.)

Reason 1:

Reason 2:

Reason 3:

Reason 4:

5. Are you persuaded that the New Testament canon is made up of the "right books" (p. 72)? Why or why not? What additional evidence would help you determine if the New Testament has the right books?

5

But Can I Trust You?

Why Trust the Bible? Summary

Throughout the centuries, scholars have accused both the disciples and the biblical authors of several shortcomings: *they're just storytellers*; *they're deceitful*; *they've been deceived themselves*; *they're confused*. As we'll see in this chapter, none of these criticisms holds water.

1. If the writers of the New Testament *aren't* trustworthy, then what are the alternatives? List and describe the four alternatives discussed on pages 82–83.

   (1)

   (2)

(3)

(4)

2. Are there any clues *in the actual text* of Scripture to suggest that the New Testament authors are *not* trying to do history? If so, where? If not, how do the Gospel authors state their purposes for writing? (See pages 83–86.)

3. Why is it exceedingly unlikely that the biblical authors are *being deceitful*? (See pages 87–91.)

4. Why is it also exceedingly unlikely that the biblical authors are *deceived themselves*? (See pages 91–96.)

5. Finally, why is it exceedingly unlikely that the biblical authors are simply *confused*? (See pages 97–100.)

6

So Did It Happen?

Why Trust the Bible? Summary
Can we have any confidence that what the writers believed happened really did happen? We can answer this question by investigating the reliability of their most important claim: Jesus's resurrection from the dead.

1. The author writes, "You can't just declare miracles—and therefore the Bible—to be implausible simply on the strength of your own experience or lack thereof" (p. 107). Why is it not necessarily implausible to believe in miracles?

2. What's wrong with the scientific objection to miracles?

3. What's wrong with the philosophical objection to miracles?

4. Lots of miracles have been recorded throughout history. Why ought we believe the Bible's and not the rest? Why are Jesus's miracles plausible?

5. The author writes, "If the resurrection happened, then the rest of the fundamental superstructure of Christianity comes together like clockwork—including the authority of the Bible, both New Testament and Old" (p. 114). Have you thought about the resurrection in this way before? Why is its truthfulness essential for Christianity?

6. Why did the disciples themselves believe in Jesus's resurrection?

7. Why can't the resurrection just be ignored?

8. From pages 118 to 121, the author lists several alternative explanations to the resurrection. List them here. Are any of them compelling to you? Why does each explanation fail?

9. What are the implications of a resurrected Jesus? List them below. (See pages 122–24.)

7

Take It on the Word of a Resurrected Man

Why Trust the Bible? Summary
Jesus got up from the dead. This changes *everything*—including how we understand both the Old and New Testaments.

Key Texts
Daniel 7:13–14
Matthew 5:17
Matthew 16:16–21
Matthew 17:22
Matthew 20:17–19
Luke 24:44
John 16:12–15
Acts 2:22–36
2 Peter 3:15–16

1. The resurrection is vital because it confirms Jesus's own claims about himself. Matthew tells us that three times Jesus predicted his own death. What do we learn through these predictions? In particular, what do they teach us about how Jesus understood his own identity as the Messiah?

2. What does the resurrection mean for the Old Testament?

3. When Jesus says things like, "You have heard it said, but I say to you," is he correcting errors in the Old Testament? If not, then what is he doing?

4. What does the resurrection mean for the New Testament? How do John 16:12–16 and 2 Peter 3:15–16 help us to answer this question?

5. So, in your own words, why should you trust the Bible?

A Final Word

The Next Question

Why Trust the Bible? Summary

Trusting the Bible is vital. But you can't really trust the Bible without also trusting whom the Bible tells you to trust: Jesus. Don't be like the Pharisees. Consider Jesus's warning to them in John 5:39–40, when he says, "You search the Scriptures because you think that in them you have eternal life; and it is they that bear witness about me, yet you refuse to come to me that you may have life." Search the Scriptures, absolutely. But then come to Jesus that you may have life.

Key Text
John 20:31

1. What have you learned by reading this book?

2. If you began this book as someone who doubted the reliability of Scripture and you *still* doubt the reliability of Scripture, what remaining objections do you have?

9Marks

Building Healthy Churches

9Marks exists to equip church leaders with a biblical vision and practical resources for displaying God's glory to the nations through healthy churches.

To that end, we want to see churches characterized by these nine marks of health:

1. Expositional Preaching
2. Gospel Doctrine
3. A Biblical Understanding of Conversion and Evangelism
4. Biblical Church Membership
5. Biblical Church Discipline
6. A Biblical Concern for Discipleship and Growth
7. Biblical Church Leadership
8. A Biblical Understanding of the Practice of Prayer
9. A Biblical Understanding and Practice of Missions

Find all our Crossway titles
and other resources at
9Marks.org.

More Study Guides from 9Marks

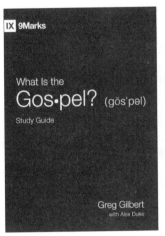

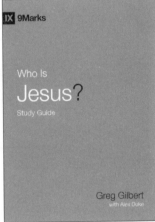

For more information, visit **crossway.org**.

NOTES

NOTES